Flying to Your Success!

Frank Basile

Charisma Publications, Inc.
Indianapolis, Indiana

Cover Art
Marti Shobett

Layout Design
Judith G. Shepherd

First Printing — August 1987
Second Printing — January 1988

ISBN 0-937008-05-2

CHARISMA PUBLICATIONS, INC.
P. O. Box 40321
Indianapolis, IN 46240
(317) 259-8743

Contents

This book contains excerpts from Frank Basile's nine books, 400 articles and 750 speeches on a variety of subjects, including motivation, goal setting, time management, human relations, sales, personal development and management.

Forward

The Rainbow In Your Life

Success is the progressive realization of your goals. Your goals should reflect your values which, in turn, are what add up to happiness for you. That is why the cover of this book depicts several symbols which could mean success depending upon your own value structure. The heart could stand for love of God, self, another person or persons, family and/or personal interests. The star could stand for recognition, ego gratification and/or authority. The dollar sign could mean career, financial and/or material achievements. The seagull is a symbol for "putting it all together" (your resources) with a positive mental attitude to accomplish whatever success means to you. It represents a positive mental attitude and all that it encompasses.

Best wishes in your flight to success!

F.M.B.

To: Marianne

SECTION I

MOTIVATIONAL

Chapter 1

Goal Setting And Motivation

Goal setting is the motivational technique designed to assist a person in getting whatever he wants out of life by effectively using his available resources. It enables him to channel his time, talent and energy directly toward specific goals. It results in greater personal and business productivity as well as a greater enjoyment of life. Life becomes more exciting and rewarding.

• • • • •

Goals help us to focus or harness our time, talent and energy. Consequently, we have fewer wasted resources. The average person may use 10% of his abilities; but with goal setting, that might increase to 20%. You may say that 20% isn't very much, *but* it's 100% more than 10%. It is the difference between just sliding by and being successful in whatever we choose.

• • • • •

Without goals, our talents and energy are disbursed. We're like a wandering generality. If we accomplish anything at all, it is by accident and probably not what we would have chosen had we consciously thought about it. However, when we have clearly defined goals, our resources are in perfect alignment. There is a clean thrust. It is like using a giant magnifying glass to focus the sun's rays on a single spot. The result is an intensity which can remove obstacles to accomplishing any goal.

● ● ● ● ●

Goal setting is an assist in getting organized. Time is not wasted on non-goal-directed activity. We know each day what needs to be done to move a little closer to our goal. We are now controlling events; they are not controlling us.

● ● ● ● ●

The way we turn on our potential is to have goals. But before we can set goals, we must decide what's important to us. Goals cover all areas of our lives, i.e., financial, spiritual, family, community, social, friends and career. Not every area will be equally important to all of us; but unless we consciously examine ourselves in all areas, we will not know their relative importance.

● ● ● ● ●

Goals give direction to our dreams and help to channel our energy and resources toward the things which we have identified as being important in our overall value structure. We are therefore more likely to achieve them. Likewise, in a business enterprise, we will more effectively use our limited resources (time, capital, manpower, equipment) when we have specific goals.

● ● ● ● ●

The key idea in goal setting is DAILY ACTION. Each goal must be supported by a detailed plan of action, which should be broken down on a daily basis. We must reduce a long term relatively non-controllable goal into something we can do every day over which we have control. We live by the day and must therefore accomplish our objectives daily.

Motivation permeates literally everything we do in every area of our lives. The extent of our motivation strongly influences how *well* we do in whatever we do and, in the final analysis, how much happiness we derive from living.

• • • • •

Motivation is not a sales rally. It is not esoteric or mysterious. It's not a big promotion. There's a lot of talk these days about motivation, but not much understanding.

• • • • •

Motivation is knowing where you want to go and how you will get there. In other words, having a goal and a plan. *Success* is the progressive realization of personal goals. *Happiness* is something to do, somebody to love and something to look forward to, which is our goals. Goals are the common denominator and are essential to happiness, success and self-motivation.

• • • • •

Motivation based upon reward or fear is external and is therefore only temporary. The strongest motivation is that which comes from within, which results from setting goals that reflect our values.

• • • • •

We are motivated and will do our best and have the most fun when we are doing something because we *want* to do it and not because of fear or reward. Webster's definition of motivation is 'that within the individual, rather than without, which incites him to action.' True motivation goes beyond the carrot and the whip to the goals a person sets for himself. These are what motivate a person to his highest potential and his greatest happiness.

The only permanent type of motivation is that which comes from within the individual. It's based on ATTITUDE. He's performing because he wants to and not because of the threat of punishment or the promise of reward. When we throw away the whip and get rid of the carrot and the stick, we may find that the donkey is actually a thoroughbred and runs because he wants to run.

● ● ● ● ●

Motivation begins with an identification of our values. Next we must select specific goals that reflect those values. We must then develop a plan of action and a timetable for implementation of each goal. Finally, we must test the goal to determine if the benefits are worth the price we must pay in terms of the action necessary to accomplish the goal. If the answer is yes, we will automatically generate the necessary desire, self-confidence and determination to carry through with the plan of action.

● ● ● ● ●

Success is different things to different people. That is why it is important that the goals we set reflect our own personal value structure. In examining our values, we should consider all areas of our life, even though not all will be equally important. We can then make conscious decisions concerning our personal priorities.

● ● ● ● ●

Success is a journey, not a destination. If we want to go from one place to another in this journey, we've got to know where it is that we want to go - our goals. These goals should reflect our values which add up to our happiness. These values are what we treasure most — love, friendship, power, fame, fortune, family, pursuit of a hobby, work, career, etc. We must determine what it is that turns us on. What it is that makes life worth living. What it is that makes us excited about getting up in the morning and looking forward to each new day as a challenge and an opportunity. We must then get moving in that direction.

We are successful when we are moving purposefully toward our desires (goals). This definition allows us to enjoy the success feeling en route (during the journey), not having to wait until some distant time when we may arrive, if ever. And when we do, we will set other goals as we travel our never ending success journey.

● ● ● ● ●

When we are pursuing goals which reflect our values, we are a success!

● ● ● ● ●

We need to determine exactly what it is that will make us happier, more satisfied, more successful. The more specific we are, the better able we are to plan to accomplish the goal.

● ● ● ● ●

When we set goals that reflect our internal value structure, we are doing those things that we most enjoy doing and are most likely to be successful and happy in their pursuit. We will take the necessary time and effort to acquire the knowledge and skills for success in that endeavor.

● ● ● ● ●

Happiness is not something we can actively pursue. It must come as a by-product of accomplishing our goals and helping other people to achieve their goals. In fact, I believe that any money we earn and any happiness we derive are only a by-product of the service we render to other human beings.

● ● ● ● ●

There is *one* quality successful salespeople have. It has nothing at all to do with age, educational background, intelligence, family history, prior experience, or physical characteristics. There is no correlation between selling success and any other factor but one. The successful salespeople are organized on a daily basis to accomplish specific goals. They are able to reduce a relatively non-controllable long term goal, i.e., earning

$60,000 for the year, to something they can do every day over which they have control, i.e., making 15-20 phone calls per day.

I've worked with drug addicts, alcoholics and other troubled in-dividuals and I know that nearly any problem can be solved to a great ex-tent by making life more meaningful through goal setting.

● ● ● ● ●

Motivation and enthusiasm must be ongoing. It is not sufficient to have a temporary boost even though it has the continuing impetus of goal setting. We must continue to feed our minds with positive input through associating with positive people, reading positive books and listening to positive tapes.

● ● ● ● ●

We should begin with short term goals so that we get immediate, posi-tive feedback and successes upon which we can build. This is why we lower the basketball net when our children are young — to give them the opportunity for success. Success breeds success, as confidence leads to greater confidence.

● ● ● ● ●

We all know people who are perpetually turned on. It's exciting to be around them. They are alive and positive. These people have goals. They have challenges in many areas of their lives.

● ● ● ● ●

It seems we are always waiting for something else to happen before we let ourselves go to do the things we have always wanted to do. But, the journey continues and it does not wait for us. Too often, we are waiting for tomorrow and for some other event to happen before we start living. We must begin *now* to consciously think of those things we want to do to make our lives more enjoyable, fulfilling, successful, etc. We must com-mit these to writing and take action now before our epitaph becomes, "He asked little of life and life paid his price."

It is not enough to dream about the things we want to do, to have or to become. We must write them down. Writing helps to crystalize our thoughts and thoughts translate into action.

● ● ● ● ●

A business owner wouldn't think of operating without a profit objective and an operating plan, which is called the budget. Yet, we spend almost no time in planning for our most precious possession, our life. We spend more time planning our vacations.

● ● ● ● ●

If we pursue goals whose benefits are greater than the price we have to pay, we will enjoy the price of success.

● ● ● ● ●

When we are away from the jungle, i.e., the everyday demands on our time, it's a good time to reflect on our values and set goals.

● ● ● ● ●

The journey of 1,000 miles begins with a single step and if we can get a person, through the vehicle of goal setting, to take that first step and taste the initial success, it may be all the impetus he needs to continue the process.

● ● ● ● ●

Motivation begins with goals. Please set one goal before you go to sleep tonight. Commit to yourself that you will do this and write it down on a 3 x 5 card. It doesn't have to be some far-reaching goal. Maybe something you have been thinking about for a while and never got around to doing. But, jut one. Not a bunch of New Year's resolutions. Keep the card in your pocket or purse as a reminder of your goal until it is accomplished; then set another. As they say, this can be the "first day of the rest of your life." The journey of a thousand miles begins with a single step. We can take that step today.

Chapter 2

Attitude

The only thing that is impossible is that which we believe is impossible. With a goal, a plan, enthusiasm and people working together as a team with a common purpose, anything is possible.

● ● ● ● ●

Greatness can be achieved — at a price. An old Spanish proverb: "Take what you want and pay for it."

● ● ● ● ●

It's all right to build your castles in the sky, but then put in the foundations!

● ● ● ● ●

Do not be afraid to make your dream list! Leaders are dreamers. The difference between our dreams and where we are now is what motivates us.

The three sides of the success triangle are SKILL, KNOWLEDGE and ATTITUDE. It's an equilateral triangle which means that all sides are equal. Any one side can limit the overall size of the triangle. In business we might put dollars in this triangle and for an individual it might be happiness or satisfaction derived from a particular endeavor. The point is that the amount of happiness, satisfaction or dollars is dependent upon the interaction of these three elements. A deficiency in any one will limit the amount of the other two that can be employed.

● ● ● ● ●

We can consciously improve our mood and attitude by acting as if we are happy and uplifted. Soon, the feeling will follow the action.

● ● ● ● ●

Emotions follow a change in behavior. Therefore if we can impact behavior, we can impact emotion. If we can impact our actions, which is what a change in behavior is, then we can impact our emotions and our feelings.

● ● ● ● ●

When behavior improves, productivity will improve along with attitude. It is not possible to directly impact attitude but the same thing can be accomplished indirectly through affecting behavior.

● ● ● ● ●

We are about as happy as we make up our minds to be. If we expect to be happy, we will be happy. Since the choice is ours, why be any other way?

Our attitude not only impacts how we feel and our own personal effectiveness but how we make others feel. Attitudes are contagious. We can help to uplift others or we can help to bring them down.

• • • • •

When we are motivated and goal directed, we will devise creative ways to offset negative situations.

• • • • •

We can change our weakness into power!

• • • • •

Every setback carries with it the seed of an equivalent or greater opportunity if we learn from the experience and make a resolution to set an alternative goal. If we will learn from defeat and move on, we can turn it into an advantage. It can be a stepping stone toward a higher goal and greater fulfillment.

• • • • •

It is not the circumstances in which we find ourselves that determine our destiny but the way we react to those circumstances. Opportunities are wherever we happen to be. The only thing holding us back is our own attitude, not the circumstances.

• • • • •

The person is a success, no matter what he is doing, if he enjoys it and derives satisfaction from it.

• • • • •

It is not our possessions nor our accomplishments which determine our happiness, but our own state of mind.

If we're not doing what we really want to do, then we'd better get out. I don't care if it's an activity, hobby, church, job, marriage or whatever. After we have given it ample opportunity and are still not doing the best we can, not liking it or being successful, we should get out. Otherwise, we'll end up in a mental institution, hospital or morgue - waiting only to stop breathing before being buried.

● ● ● ● ●

Before we can acquire or accomplish anything of significance, we must first become. We must become the type of person who deserves to own the thing that we want.

● ● ● ● ●

Before we can accomplish or become anything, we must first determine "why." Why do we want to accomplish, or to become? For our family, ourselves, recognition, money, power, additional leisure time, etc? The "how" doesn't make any difference until we determine the "why." The "why" provides the inspiration and the motivation.

● ● ● ● ●

Positive programming results in positive habit patterns. We can take control of our programming and, therefore, our habits.

● ● ● ● ●

By programming our subconscious for good and not evil, for success and not failure, with positives instead of negatives, we are taking a giant step toward our own success and happiness. This is one of the great uses of affirmations, such as the poem "New Day," which I recite every morning.

Writing helps to crystalize our thoughts and thoughts translate into action. We must first mentally accomplish before we can physically accomplish. Thought precedes action.

• • • • •

Each of us will get exactly what we expect. If we expect positive, we will get it. If we expect negative, we will get it. I don't mean giving lip service to it; I mean really *expecting* it. Therefore, to attract positive responses and rewards, we must think and act positively.

• • • • •

Affirmations help program the subconscious. Most of us have been handicapped by negative programming as we matured. The only way to counteract that negative conditioning is to substitute positive conditioning in its place.

• • • • •

Why not live every day like it's your last, and like it's the last day of those you love. One day it will. See if you don't have a few more minutes to stop and talk with someone who may need a word of encouragement from you, or an employee who needs some advice or your son or daughter who wants to tell you about what happened that day.

• • • • •

Why the head long dash to get as much done as possible? Slow down and live. That's not to say that you should not have goals and action plans. Your life should have balance, with goals in all areas which you consider significant. But, why take the journey if you can't enjoy it?

Concentrate on the task at hand to maximize the use of your brain power.

• • • • •

Charisma is that quality that makes some people more popular than others. They have a type of mystical attraction and exercise control or influence over others.

• • • • •

In a study of one of the top brokerage firms, I found that 20% of the salespeople sold 80% of the real estate. I can't prove this next statement, but I have a feeling it is true. Twenty percent of the people in *life* get 80% of the action, however we define action in our individual definition of success.

• • • • •

Smile. A smile says a thousand things to another person — that you are pleased with where you are, who you are, the person you are with and what you are doing. It not only makes you feel good but radiates and transmits that enthusiasm to others.

• • • • •

Unless there is an attitude change, nothing will happen any differently after training than before. If the participants have been in a business for any period of time, they are not going to learn much new. They already know what they are doing wrong. They must resolve that they will take specific action as a result of the training.

• • • • •

Studies show that 90% of all illnesses have psychosomatic origins. The way we think affects the way we feel and the general state of our physical health. In other words, we can think ourselves sick or healthy.

Doctors are now joining with therapists and others in treating the whole person and not merely a portion of the person which might contain only the symptom of the problem. For example, they are not simply treating the leg because it aches, but also the mind because it could be causing the leg to ache.

● ● ● ● ●

Attitude impacts our physical well-being and fits under the general umbrella of the holistic approach. A study at the University of Chicago showed that healthy people apparently have in common a certain "hardiness" — a set of personality traits that protects them from stress. Their attitude toward stressful events is much more important than the events themselves. One can experience stress and either become ill or stay healthy — depending upon attitude.

Putting it all together

SECTION II

PERSONAL

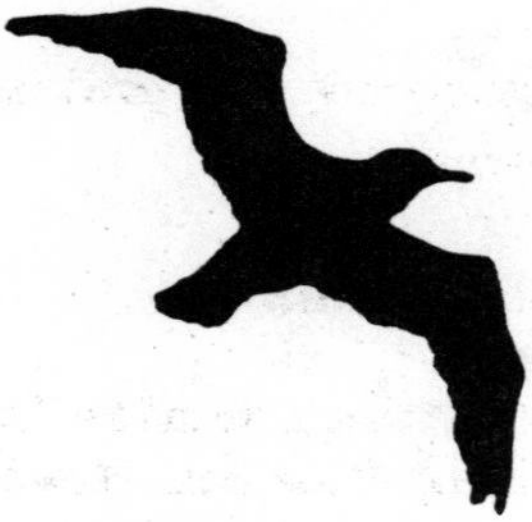

Chapter 3

Personal Development

Continue to grow personally and professionally. Make a self-development plan and stick to it.

• • • • •

Most of us have always been advised to "lead with your strength", which is appropriate in many situations. However, it is sometimes appropriate to lead with your weakness and to save your strength for the grand finale.

• • • • •

I attempt to have unity in all of my activities which means that a given action will have a multiple or ripple effect. For example, I will write a company procedure which will in turn become a published article, a segment of a seminar and a portion of a book. The act of researching and writing the procedure will, therefore, have many ripple benefits in addition to serving as a procedure to streamline company operations.

Patience is having something else to do while you are waiting. That is why it is important to have many irons in the fire. You will not be anxiously awaiting the outcome of a single project. Everything will not, therefore, "all hang in the balance" and all of your time and emotion will not be spent worrying and awaiting the outcome of only one pursuit. If that were the case, time would pass very slowly and you would accomplish nothing in the interim, worrying about the outcome of that project.

● ● ● ● ●

Have many goals and interests so you do not place excessive importance on any one. As a side benefit, a setback in one area will not devastate you. Chances are you will have a high percentage of wins.

● ● ● ● ●

We miss 75% of what is happening in our lives unless we concentrate, listen and cultivate an awareness of what is happening to and around us.

● ● ● ● ●

Know yourself, like yourself and be yourself. We cannot like ourselves or be ourselves unless we first know ourselves.

● ● ● ● ●

Let me see, really see, the people with whom I work, play and otherwise associate. Let me see their dreams, aspirations and feelings and have compassion and empathy. Even more important, let me understand my own feelings and moods.

● ● ● ● ●

Sometimes we don't take the time or effort to be aware of ourselves, the people around us or our general situation. We go through life in a zombie-like state, neither feeling nor caring nor really knowing.

Chapter 4

Training

A lot of what I teach came about through my own personal experience, which is one way to learn. But it isn't the best way. When we try to learn everything first hand, we are needlessly re-inventing the wheel and taking longer than we should to accomplish the job.

●●●●●

Formal training, whether presented through a university course or within the context of individual workshops or seminars, is important. It is more economical to learn through OPE (other people's experiences) than through making the mistakes ourselves. That can be quite expensive. Sometimes we go broke in the process. The tuition in the school of hard knocks is much more expensive than formalized training.

●●●●●

Sharing information helps to reinforce it in our own mind and heart.

●●●●●

The problem with most motivational seminars is that they have a temporary uplifting effect upon the participants but no carryover, lasting impact unless some action is taken to sustain the enthusiasm. If participants set their goals immediately after the program, that will give them the impetus to continue their enthusiasm because of their desire to achieve their goals. Once that goal is achieved, the resulting success feeling, as well as the additional enthusiasm, will hopefully encourage them to continue goal setting.

● ● ● ● ●

We learn through repetition but we learn even faster when we take action. Therefore, if people get into motion quickly on the goal setting technique, the chances of their carrying it into their everyday lives is much greater. The end product of any education is to stimulate action in the direction of that education. We are much more likely to take action when we take the first step as part of the program itself.

● ● ● ● ●

The real pay-off of any educational program comes from doing something a little different than what would have been done had it not been for the program. That difference is the goal. Unless the means or device is provided to make it easy for the participants to set goals, the likelihood of their taking any action is practically nil. In fact, people will forget 90% of what was covered in the program unless they take immediate action on the ideas presented or unless they are exposed to repetition.

● ● ● ● ●

People change themselves through goal setting with a little help from an agent who motivates them to recognize their values and set goals. People need guidance to begin this process. If we can somehow motivate a person to analyze his values and set goals, he will do the rest.

Chapter 5

Personality Styles

Understanding the personality types of others and how to deal with each will assist us in many ways, including human relations, recruiting, management development, managing, selling, communicating and team building.

● ● ● ● ●

A knowledge and understanding of our own behavioral style is the first step in learning how to become more effective and successful through changing our style or portions of it and/or adapting our style in various situations.

● ● ● ● ●

When we consciously study behavior and understand the styles of others, we can adapt our style and method of management to help others feel more comfortable.

● ● ● ● ●

A successful national property management organization in Los Angeles teaches its supervisory personnel that there are three essential characteristics for success. One of these is flexibility – being able to adapt management and personality styles to be most effective with subordinates and others within the company.

• • • • •

An article in PSYCHOLOGY TODAY provided the results of a study of successful salespeople. They found that the successful salesperson is able to adapt both his personality style and presentation to match that of the prospect. In other words, he is able to make the prospect feel as comfortable as possible so that he is most likely to agree with the salesperson.

• • • • •

When we recognize and understand the behavioral styles of others, we will then be able to identify areas of possible interpersonal conflict so that these can be minimized or avoided entirely.

• • • • •

By understanding personality styles, we are better able to match those that are compatible from both the standpoint of productivity and human relations. If we cannot achieve a perfect match, we are at least aware of the potential conflicts.

• • • • •

The better we understand ourselves and the other person, the more effective the communication will be.

• • • • •

When we understand the work styles of our employees in relation to what is required for job success we can make recommendations on how they can become more effective, i.e., capitalize on strengths, minimize weaknesses, take a course on certain subjects or simply be alert to certain natural tendencies and try to change or alter them either permanently or in certain situations. Understanding our employees' work styles helps us in developing them.

● ● ● ● ●

As an important by-product of measuring a person's personal characteristics in the hiring process, we will be able to more effectively manage him on an ongoing basis to ensure maximum productivity and job satisfaction. While we can't directly motivate another person, we can create the environment which is conducive to his success. We are not all motivated in the same way.

Chapter 6

Human Relations

Human relations is the art of getting along with people.

●●●●●

Since people are interested in themselves, there is no better way to get a person's attention than by directing the conversation toward those things that matter most to him. This principle applies whether you are trying to get someone to like you, persuade him and/or change his behavior.

●●●●●

The key idea in human relations is IMPORTANT. The need to feel important is the greatest craving that human beings have. When we can help another person have a better opinion of himself by helping him to feel important, he is more likely to like us and do that which we want. This applies equally to our employees, employers, peers, customers, family, etc. We help another person feel important by talking in terms of his interests, listening to him, providing sincere recognition, etc.

The better we can help another person feel about himself the more likely he is to do that which we want him to do.

• • • • •

Be a good listener. Encourage others to talk about themselves. Not only should you talk in terms of the other person's interests but you should encourage the other person to talk about himself and what interests him and then *listen*. This does not mean passive but *active* listening where you respond both verbally and non-verbally to what is said so that the person feels and believes that you are taking an active interest in what he is saying.

• • • • •

Remember and use the other person's name. Memory is a skill which can be improved through concentration, repetition and association.

• • • • •

There is value in showing one's humanity or vulnerability. People can somehow better identify and feel warmer toward a person when they realize he is not "perfect." People do not like to think that another person is perfect. They like to know that we all have flaws.

• • • • •

I recall a survey in which women were asked what they liked most in men. I was surprised that "vulnerability" ranked very high in the desired traits.

• • • • •

Always be careful to determine the *real* reason why someone is doing something or making or refusing a request. This applies in both personal and business situations.

When someone says he wants to do something because of, then adds *in addition to* or *besides*, listen very carefully because what follows is the real reason.

● ● ● ● ●

There are always at least two reasons for doing anything — the first one and the real reason. If you are too quick to accept or refute the first reason and do not restrain yourself sufficiently to listen while the person continues to talk, or you do not ask additional probing questions, you may miss the real reason and act upon a secondary motivation — not the true one.

● ● ● ● ●

Use as little force as possible to accomplish your objective. Don't go for overkill. It's a waste of resources and tends to breed resentment. Don't worry about winning by an exorbitant margin; just simply win. Always allow the other person to save face. Why bury your opponent? Resist the killer instinct. Use judgment and compassion in dealing with another person.

● ● ● ● ●

When dealing with another person, if you have to put down his argument to win the case, do it as gently as possible and with no more ammunition than you need to accomplish your objective. Don't unnecessarily damage his argument or his self-esteem, or both.

● ● ● ● ●

When you are having an argument, don't throw in everything possible, like anything that has ever occurred with the other individual, to prove your point. If the argument is over a minor issue, don't drop atomic bombs. You do more damage than what would have occurred by simply engaging in the minor argument. Don't use a machine gun to kill a fly!

Too often, unfortunately, we "gunny sack" many grievances against another person and explode them all at the same time. Usually it is sparked by some trivial matter or disagreement. We may never undo the harm which is thereby done by unleashing a vicious attack.

● ● ● ● ●

Often, we could wait awhile when we have to tell someone "no." Circumstances may take care of it. The idea or request may prove to be impractical, the person may change his mind or some other occurrence will preclude the "no" or the "no" may become unnecessary for some other reason. On the other hand, don't unnecessarily delay the "no" if the delay would interfere with your, or another person's, efficiency or would be deceiving.

Chapter 7

Self-esteem

Self-esteem is how we feel about ourselves. It is an emotion. It is not egotism or trying to prove our self-worth by what we own or wear. This generally reflects low self-esteem.

● ● ● ● ●

Genuinely enjoy yourself in a wide variety of activities involving work, play, creative self-expression, companionship or just plain loafing.

● ● ● ● ●

When you are speaking with people, look them directly in the eye. This is a clear indication of the degree of a person's self-confidence.

● ● ● ● ●

Become more self-assertive. Reduce your compliance to others and express your own needs and wishes in a definite way.

Be your own person. Do not attempt to dominate others, and likewise don't allow others to dominate you. Recognize the uniqueness in others as well as in yourself.

• • • • •

The only person you must really face is the guy in the glass. More than anyone else, he will know whether your actions are in congruence with your underlying belief structure and whether they represent your true potential.

• • • • •

Rely upon your own judgment regarding your actions and what you do. Do not constantly seek the approval of others such as your parents, minister, friends, co-workers, boss, etc. No one else is exactly on your wavelength. Seek appropriate advice and counsel, but you make the final decisions concerning your life.

• • • • •

Set goals which reflect your basic values and develop a plan of action for each. This will do as much as anything else to enhance your self-image by improving your self-confidence. You are self-confident when you know where you are going and how you are going to get there. You will be among the few who do.

• • • • •

If you don't already have them, develop a strong set of beliefs which you are willing to defend and which forms the underlying values for your goals. However, you must be secure enough within yourself to modify those beliefs if evidence indicates that they should be changed.

Often, your "acres of diamonds" is right where you are now and not in some distant future, or in some other territory or career where the grass might appear greener. You cannot have high self-esteem if you are constantly discontent with your present conditions. Change them, if you will, but don't needlessly fret and worry.

● ● ● ● ●

To say that you should accept yourself does not mean you should not continually strive to improve.

● ● ● ● ●

Persons with a healthy self-esteem know themselves and like themselves and are not continually comparing themselves, generally unfavorably, with others. This is a no win proposition. Each of us is a unique human being with an opportunity to make our own unique contributions.

● ● ● ● ●

Accept yourself the way you are and improve upon your weaknesses and reinforce your strengths. Don't compare yourself with others. Set your own standards and go for them.

● ● ● ● ●

Think of all of your good qualities and the things and people you have to be thankful for. These will help to reinforce your self-esteem.

● ● ● ● ●

Gracefully accept compliments by saying "thank you" instead of putting yourself down. An indication of a person's self-esteem is the manner in which he accepts a compliment. Those with low self-esteem will tend to deflect a compliment with such comments as, "Oh, it was nothing.

I just got lucky." Those with a healthy self-esteem will accept the compliment and not devalue it.

• • • • •

Eliminate those people from your life who are constantly putting you down, calling attention to your shortcomings and weaknesses and, in general, devaluing you as a human being and therefore having an adverse effect on your self-esteem. Instead, surround yourself with positive people who help to build your self-image and self-esteem. These may be people who understand your faults and shortcomings, but who like you anyway and who help you to overcome these. They do not use them as a weapon against you.

• • • • •

Praise and compliment yourself as well as others. Recognition is vital to growth and self-esteem. When you can help another person have a better opinion of himself through recognizing his positive contributions and actions, you are doing him a great service. You are affirming his self-worth. You are not only reinforcing his positive action, but also improving his attitude about himself, you and the company. This will result in better performance, more praise, greater compensation, etc.

• • • • •

The words you speak about yourself not only influence the way others perceive you but, most importantly, how you perceive and feel about yourself. These words can either reinforce your self-esteem if they are positive or lower your self-esteem if they are "put-down" words. When your thoughts and words are positive, your self-esteem is improved and you tend toward positive action which then leads to higher self-esteem, more accomplishment, etc. You have a benign cycle. Unfortunately, the reverse also happens.

Words have a tremendous impact upon our self-esteem. The constant negative bombardment from parents and teachers, as well as from the environment and the media, can take its toll.

• • • • •

Unfortunately, most of us were handicapped from the beginning with low self-esteem. It was transmitted, unwittingly, by our parents in the words they used to describe us or our actions, which we took as personal reflections on our worth as a person. They told us how thoughtless we were, how we failed to do our chores around the house, how forgetful, how ungrateful, etc.

• • • • •

Do not constantly look toward tomorrow or backwards toward yesterday but live today the best you can. Today may be all you have and what you make of today determines how you live your life and the degree of happiness you enjoy.

• • • • •

Separate your actions, especially your failures, from your essence and value as a human being. Because you may have failed does not mean you are a failure. You must be able to recognize the difference in yourself and in others.

• • • • •

Savor and remember your successes and victories because they tend to improve your self-esteem. Remember how and why you achieved those successes so that this can be reinforced and used in the future.

Learn from your failures and setbacks so that you do not repeat them but then banish them from your memory. They only serve to lower your self-esteem and to make you feel bad.

$$\bullet \ \bullet \ \bullet \ \bullet \ \bullet$$

It is important that we get the success feeling when we are young because this is when our self-esteem is the most fragile. Winning then helps to motivate us to continue to improve. This has a carry-over effect into all areas of our lives and provides us with a feeling of self-confidence upon which we can build through a lifetime. It is then important to build upon this initial base and to constantly adjust our sights and goals upward. This will ensure a continuation of a success-oriented, positive philosophy.

$$\bullet \ \bullet \ \bullet \ \bullet \ \bullet$$

People with high self-esteem accomplish more, are happier, and are a more positive influence on their family members and co-workers. As managers, it is therefore important that our employees, as well as ourselves, have high self-esteem.

$$\bullet \ \bullet \ \bullet \ \bullet \ \bullet$$

Without a healthy self-esteem, it is almost impossible to achieve success or happiness.

$$\bullet \ \bullet \ \bullet \ \bullet \ \bullet$$

Persons with low self-esteem seek ways to escape from reality such as promiscuity, drugs, drinking and anger toward others. Studies have shown that low self-esteem is the root cause of practically every personal problem and breeds anxiety and fear. It prevents friendships and loving relationships. It causes harsh judgments of others and oneself. Unfortunately, it is passed on to one's children.

A recent Gallup poll found that, on the average, 37% of Americans have high self-esteem, 33% average and 30% low. Interestingly, those with low self-esteem reported more symptoms of stress and poor health while placing more importance on material things such as achievement and success at work. Those in the high group tended to place more emphasis in their lives on the importance of maintaining a healthy mind, a good family life, a balanced outlook; they equate success more with happiness than with material gains.

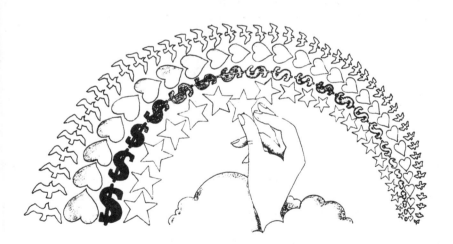

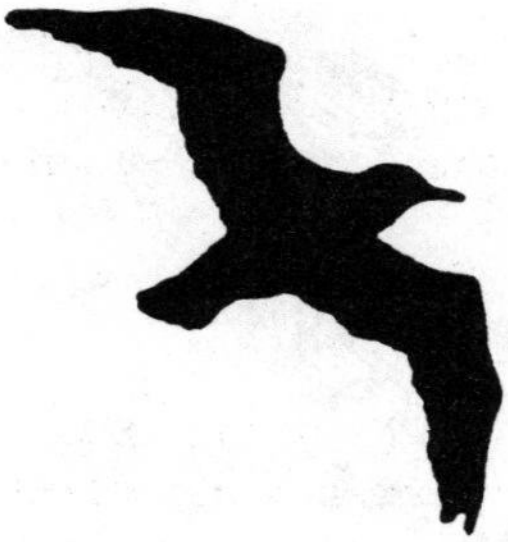

Chapter 8

Image

People judge us in only four ways – how we look, what we do, what we say and how we say it. How we look is the critical first impression and we never have a second chance to make a good first impression.

● ● ● ● ●

Appearance is important not only because it is how other people judge us but, even more importantly, because of its impact upon our own self image. We feel better about ourselves when we look good. Therefore, a person benefits in two ways because of good appearance. One is external – how it impacts other people, and the other is internal – how it impacts our own self-esteem. Both of these positively affect self-confidence and performance.

● ● ● ● ●

Dress and look your best. It will help you to feel better about yourself and motivate others to feel better about you. It also helps you to succeed because first impressions are critical to success. You also tend to walk better, feel better and project better when you look good.

All of us are becoming more image conscious as we realize the importance of the image we project, not only to the way others perceive us, but to the way we feel about ourselves and therefore how we perform.

● ● ● ● ●

Image is as important in determining our success as is our ability and effort. Therefore, it behooves each of us to consider carefully how to cultivate an image designed to achieve and become whatever it is that we want.

● ● ● ● ●

We must consciously market ourselves almost as we would market a product. How can we become more marketable? Through enhancing and honing our image. As a by-product, we'll also be happier because generally those areas that add to our image are also those which make us feel better about ourselves and show better care and attention to our bodies and appearance.

● ● ● ● ●

Our appearance can frequently make the difference between letting an opportunity slip away and getting a second interview. Unfortunately, a person's real potential may not be discovered because of an initial judgement based upon appearance.

Chapter 9

Worry And Stress

Every difficulty carries with it the seed of a greater opportunity if we will only recognize it and take action. This can help us to overcome the down feeling that results from a difficulty.

● ● ● ● ●

No matter how bleak things seem to be, we can turn them to our advantage, especially if we receive a little help, encouragement or support. It can mean the difference between tragedy and success.

● ● ● ● ●

Determine the worst thing that can happen from a situation. Decide that you will accept that if necessary. As soon as you have mentally accepted the worst that can happen, a certain release occurs. You can then take constructive action to improve upon that.

● ● ● ● ●

Calculate how much worry something is worth. Don't give it a minute more. Move on.

Don't dwell on a negative occurrence. Decide what, if anything, you can do and take immediate action or schedule action for a later time if it cannot be taken at once. Then move on to something else.

● ● ● ● ●

Think of all the reasons why an unfortunate event may be the best thing that could have happened. Initially, you may have to do a little "con-.ning" to convince yourself. However, once convinced, you can take action to make that come true. You can set an alternate goal, which goal is better than the one you would have achieved had the unfortunate incident not occurred. Look for the best in that situation and exploit it.

● ● ● ● ●

Generally, you can overcome a temporary down condition or setback and again become uplifted and positive. If it is an ongoing condition, professional help may be called for. My philosophy, however, is that you *can* control your feelings and emotions.

● ● ● ● ●

A manager, like anyone else, is subject to worry and/or "getting down." This can adversely affect productivity. He cannot be most effective when he is worried or depressed.

● ● ● ● ●

Most of our ills could be eliminated by positive, healthy thinking.

● ● ● ● ●

Try changing something about you, perhaps your appearance, or about what you do. Try a new hairdo or let your beard grow. Treat yourself to a leisurely bubble bath. Do something different. Maybe something a little silly. It might just change your whole outlook. Change something; change anything.

• • • • •

Improvement in exercise, diet and/or sleep could be the key to revitalization if one or more of these is lacking. There are excellent books on all three subjects which can provide professional guidance for self-help in these areas.

• • • • •

Sometimes merely venting your feelings and emotions about a personal or business situation or problem can ease your mind and make you feel better.

• • • • •

I believe a person tends toward being positive and mentally healthy without any outside intervention. Often, a talk with a supportive, non-judgmental confidante can be good therapy, uplifting you out of the doldrums. Perhaps the confidante can shed a little light on the situation – showing that it can be solved, it is not as difficult or as serious as you thought, or it is needless to worry about something you cannot control.

• • • • •

What is sunk is gone and we cannot do anything about it. All that matters is what we can do from now on. That is what we should concentrate upon. It's the marginal that counts. Whenever I start to brood, I write "marginal" on a sheet of paper. That helps to dismiss the worry from my mind or, as a minimum, put it into proper perspective.

We often destroy today's happiness by worrying about things which have already occurred or which may possibly occur at some future time. We fail to live constructively in the present and to enjoy the moment. Learn your lessons from past mistakes but don't dwell on them.

• • • • •

Take life one day at a time. Too often the things which drive you to depression are the things you are anticipating that may or may not happen and over which you may or may not have any control. If you have control, you should work at doing something about it, which work itself will help overcome the depression. Anticipate problems and prepare for their solutions, but don't spend time needlessly worrying about them. If you can do nothing about them, there is no point in worrying. Cooperate with the inevitable, relax and don't get uptight over a situation you cannot control or change. Also, 80% of those things you worry about never actually happen.

• • • • •

Concentrate on your goals because they reflect that which is important to you. These are the positives in your life — the reasons why you get up in the morning. It is difficult for a person to focus on the positives if he has never taken the time to determine what those positives (goals) are, i.e., what he is living for. It is then easy for the least setback or negative situation to throw him into a depression. Keeping your time and energy focused on the plan for accomplishing your goals will leave little time for negative emotions.

• • • • •

Count your blessings. Fill your mind with positive thoughts about your accomplishments and the good people and things in your life. Focus on the positives and not on the unfortunate occurrence which is causing your depression. The positives will almost always outweigh the negatives. You generally tend to lose sight of these when a negative situation occurs.

You may choose to become depressed, angry, resentful, envious and all of the other reactions and feelings which throw you into a depression and keep you in a "down" condition. Or, you may choose to be happy, helpful, forgiving and all of the positive emotions and feelings that pick you up and keep you there.

● ● ● ● ●

Happiness is a state of mind and not the result of your condition or circumstance. You cannot always control your circumstances or environment. You can, however, control how you react to those circumstances and, therefore, how you feel.

● ● ● ● ●

Self-image is an important ingredient in maintaining an "up" attitude. It is difficult to be positive about anything else when you are not positive about yourself.

● ● ● ● ●

Stress, especially job related stress, has been found to be the leading cause of long term depression, anxiety, alcoholism and drug addiction.

● ● ● ● ●

Physical and emotional fitness is conducive to effective mental effort. If a high level of stress is detrimental to health, it follows that it is also likely to have an adverse impact on job performance, whether caused by personal or work related reasons.

Chapter 10

Determination

If we are going to lose weight, we can't diet once in a while; we must diet every day. If we are going to become conditioned for a marathon race, we can't practice just weekly or monthly; we must practice daily.

● ● ● ● ●

Success does not come in big chunks, but in small, sometimes minute, doses. Some of the *rewards* may come at intervals, i.e., recognition, winning a race or prize, getting a raise, etc., but the effort required to achieve those rewards is expended daily.

● ● ● ● ●

Success does not come overnight but as a result of constant, daily application and work.

● ● ● ● ●

Leaders do things that people rarely see and which don't make headlines, and which are not romantic or leaderesque — such as the constant study required to keep up with what is going on in an organization and the world (as it might impact the organization). They don't realize the myriad of reports which must be read, digested and acted upon, or the countless encounters with employees, peers, industry associates, the media, etc., which require doing things right. This daily activity is what builds a leader's record and reputation and eventually forms a strong leadership pattern.

•••••

All of the little actions, which together make us a leader, occur in slices on an ongoing basis. To paraphrase the late Vince Lombardi, winning is doing things right, not once in a while, or from time to time, but every day, in every way, in every minute of every game. Sure, we will have our big moments, but these are generally the result of daily plodding toward our objectives.

•••••

The years are comprised of months, the months of weeks, the weeks of days, the days of hours and the hours of minutes. Habits, reputations and records are compiled and reinforced continuously - every minute of every day.

•••••

We live by the day, not by the week or month or year. We have no control over what's going to happen tomorrow or next week or next month and there is no point in worrying over what happened yesterday, except to learn from it. The only time over which we have any control is now.

•••••

Success requires going back to the basics. It means properly learning the basics of whatever business we are in and practicing them day in and day out. Success may seem a long time coming but it *will* come.

There are many examples of people who have achieved outstanding success only after years of work and effort.

● ● ● ● ●

How many of us have thrown in the towel because success seemed to take too long? Success doesn't come overnight. We must be willing to hang tough and to grind it out. If you can take it, you can make it.

SECTION III

COMMUNICATIONS

Chapter 11

Speaking

Since how we speak is 25% of how we are judged, it is important that we speak well – not only in one-to-one conversation but also within a group setting. As we move higher on the organizational ladder, this skill becomes even more important. It is a skill which is worth learning and developing.

• • • • •

The Book of Lists, Volume 1, lists speaking in public as the number one fear of the 14 greatest fears. Death ranked number two! What is the source of this fear? The UNKNOWN! We fear that which we do not know. To overcome this fear, the unknown must become known and this is accomplished through knowledge and practice.

• • • • •

The March, 1983 edition of SUCCESS Magazine, in a special article about career changes, said there are six "highly transferrable skills most employers look for in hiring people." Public speaking ranked number one, followed by budget management, managing/supervising, interviewing, instructing and writing. Four of the six involve communications.

There are two main reasons for taking the time to study and/or review the basics of speaking. One is necessity. The need to speak clearly and forcefully is invaluable in achieving success in business or professional endeavors. Anyone involved in business is subject to being asked to "say a few words," chair a meeting and/or participate in a meeting. Another reason is enjoyment. Intelligent study of speaking for use in business or social life brings pleasures of various kinds which constantly increase as you become more expert.

● ● ● ● ●

Speaking is magnified conversation. Instead of speaking one-to-one, it is one-to-many. We can simulate one-to-one conversation by focusing on one person at a time instead of looking at the audience as a group.

● ● ● ● ●

Many of us do not speak well because we have fragile self-esteem. We are afraid to appear foolish in front of others. When we become more confident and let go of our vanity, the fear will lessen.

● ● ● ● ●

The best material for our speeches results from our own personal experiences. This is the source for relevant stories which help to support the points we make.

● ● ● ● ●

People like stories. Stories help to visualize the message in an interesting and memorable way. They are much more likely to remember what we say and to retain it when they receive the message reinforced by an illustration or story.

If we are a product of the product in what we are speaking about, and we should be, then our experience should provide significant stories or vignettes to illustrate our points. One caution is important. Avoid the trap of becoming the hero in each example. We should be able to use some examples to show our own failure, at least in the beginning, and how we perhaps overcame a weakness or a failure by using the principles we are discussing.

• • • • •

Stories rooted in our own personal experience lend themselves best to our own personal style and allow us to relate them with feeling. They are also easiest to recall. When we are attempting to relate straight information, it is more difficult to remember and we generally have to stick closer to our notes.

• • • • •

We should not sleepwalk through life, but rather be aware of ourselves and what's happening to us and how it can relate to other things in which we are interested. We can then see how routine daily happenings can be used to illustrate points we are making.

• • • • •

We must develop an awareness in order to recognize how an experience could relate to our subject, an upcoming talk or meeting or perhaps be filed for future use.

• • • • •

As time goes on, we accumulate hundreds of vignettes which may be anywhere from a minute to an hour each. These form the basis for our talks and are our mental reservoir for, perhaps, responding to questions during a workshop. People then become amazed at how we can immediately respond and "make up" a speech on the spur of the moment.

Once when I gave a so-called spontaneous 45-minute talk, everyone was amazed at how well it came off. What they did not realize was that I had been preparing for that talk for over 10 years, ever since I was involved in speaking. I merely put a series of vignettes in the proper sequence and bridged logically to each one to support the points I was making. Any speaker, after awhile, with any sense of awareness and a filing system which permits retrieval, would be able to accomplish this "amazing" task.

● ● ● ● ●

Someone will occasionally say to me, "I wish I could speak like you do. I would give anything." If that were true, they would give over 100 speeches a year (at least two per week), read books and articles and listen *regularly* to tapes about speaking. They would subscribe to newsletters on the art of speaking and belong to the National Speakers Association and attend their educational sessions. In summary, they would pay the price for being a good speaker by studying, preparing and practicing on an ongoing basis. Becoming skillful at anything requires regular application.

● ● ● ● ●

Occasionally, someone will say, "It is easy for you because you have a gift of gab." It is not a gift! It has resulted from many years of study, practice and preparation.

Chapter 12

Humor

In his book ANATOMY OF AN ILLNESS, Norman Cousins described how humor helped to cure him of an "incurable" disease. We will not only live longer but will also be happier when we inject humor into our everyday lives. It is good for us personally, professionally, physically and psychologically.

• • • • •

People often use humor to accomplish their objectives, i.e., managers, lovers, salespeople, politicians, etc. It has been effectively used to sell people, products and ideas. In fact, television advertising makes extensive use of humor.

• • • • •

Humor can be used to destroy people and ideas. The cutting joke can be more devastating than a mountain of statistics and facts against an idea or person.

• • • • •

Humor can backfire if it is not appropriate or if it is in bad taste, i.e., telling an off-color story to the wrong audience or, in my opinion, to any audience. Also, humor used for the purpose of attacking someone could be a two-edged sword, especially if the other person comes back with a witty retort.

● ● ● ● ●

Humor can also be used to show that a situation is under control. An example is President Reagan's remark after the assassination attempt several years ago, "I forgot to duck." This reassured the nation that he was still in charge.

● ● ● ● ●

In business, humor can be employed in a one-on-one discussion with another person, in a meeting or when delivering a speech.

● ● ● ● ●

Each of us has been involved at one time or another in a meeting where humor "saved the day." Perhaps it was an awkward moment with a subordinate or the boss. Maybe it was during an argument with one's spouse. An appropriate, well-placed humorous comment can reduce tension, relax people, diffuse anger, change attitudes, lighten an embarrassing situation, refute an argument, create an image, or restore goodwill.

● ● ● ● ●

Speakers know how important humor can be to their profession. They generally use humor to begin a talk because it puts the audience at ease, reduces tension (including the speaker's), and helps to win the audience over at the start. We like people who can make us laugh.

Humor can be used to change pace when the speaker senses that he may be losing part of the audience. It gives people a "mental break." As in general conversation, it can effectively drive home a point. However, the humor should be appropriate to the speaker, audience and the occasion; it should not be "off the wall."

● ● ● ● ●

There is an old saying in the speaking profession that you don't have to use humor, "only if you want to get paid." Most of the top speakers include some humor in their messages. People do not want to be lectured to; they want to be entertained. In some cases, you must slip the message between the entertainment.

Chapter 13

Listening

Listening is a skill. It can be improved through training and practice, just as with reading, writing and speaking.

● ● ● ● ●

We don't learn when we are speaking, only when we listen.

● ● ● ● ●

Listening is vital in human relations.

● ● ● ● ●

There is no better way to get what we want, to get the other person to like us or to change him in some way, than for him to talk and for us to listen.

● ● ● ● ●

Listening helps the other person feel important. Therefore, he is bound to feel good about us.

Listening is important if we are to remember and use a person's name. Usually, we are thinking about what we are going to say in response to the introduction instead of concentrating on the person and his name.

● ● ● ● ●

We sell by asking questions and listening. This is called qualifying. We are asking the other person questions to help us understand his needs so we can show how our product or service satisfies those needs. If we don't listen after we ask questions, we will not be able to sell effectively.

● ● ● ● ●

Often, we don't allow a prospect to fully answer a question. Sometimes we even anticipate his answer and jump in with a reply. The best advice ever given to a salesperson who asked the closing question (asked the prospect to buy) is to SHUT UP. The next person to speak, after the closing question is asked, loses. This applies not only to selling, but to negotiating.

● ● ● ● ●

Many of us have the tendency to interrupt while another person is talking. We don't make the person feel good or important when we don't give him an opportunity to be fully heard.

● ● ● ● ●

Listening is important in complaint handling. We tend to become defensive after the customer's initial statement. However, if we allow the angry person to vent his feelings, often this is all that he really wants – to be heard. Just listening will help to diffuse the anger. At worst, it allows us to fully understand the problem. Immediately attempting to respond to the first statement of a complaint will only aggravate the person even more. He will want to justify his position. If the complaint is not legitimate, he may even realize that it does not make sense if we allow him to speak it and repeat it.

As opposed to *passive* listening, *active* listening is when we sit up, occasionally lean forward, ask pertinent questions, look at the person and, in general, show that we are interested in what he is saying. We want to hear *and* see what is being communicated so that we can pick up the nonverbal signals which are critical to a full understanding of the sender's message.

Chapter 14

Body Language

Body language is an art, not a science. Gestures are clues to what is being communicated and not concrete evidence. It is necessary to get confirmation and feedback to verify our tentative conclusions.

● ● ● ● ●

If we are not aware of a person's body language, we may miss the meaning of the communication and react inappropriately.

● ● ● ● ●

To get the full meaning in any communication requires that we be observant and listen with our eyes.

● ● ● ● ●

In a typical conversation, 70% of what is being communicated is nonverbal. It is the nonverbal which reflects a person's true feelings and attitudes.

61

Words generally portray a person's role but his gestures reveal his underlying motivations which might be on a subconscious level. Gestures provide insight into the person's instinctive reactions to what is being said or the situation. It is an accurate reflection of what people are thinking.

• • • • •

If there is a conflict between the verbal and the nonverbal, generally the nonverbal is more accurate. An example is the nervous laugh. The sound itself is one of amusement, but the nervousness reveals that the person is uncomfortable and the laugh is probably a coverup. There is a Cantonese proverb which says, "Watch out for the man whose stomach doesn't move when he laughs."

• • • • •

We must learn to read gestures which may or may not be consistent with the spoken word. In fact, the gestures may not even be consistent with one another. It takes study and skill to determine the true meaning when there are conflicting individual gestures within a cluster.

• • • • •

We should consider not only the verbal and nonverbal signals but also the situation, the people involved and circumstances. We do not communicate in a vacuum.

• • • • •

People may not be able to, or even want to, put into words what they mean or feel. Their gestures, either consciously or unconsciously, will reveal their feelings to the observant person.

Skill in reading body language can be extremely useful in managing, selling, negotiating, screening and hiring, socializing and speaking.

● ● ● ● ●

In addition to better understanding what the other person is communicating through his gestures, it is important for us to understand body language to ensure that our gestures are communicating what we want to convey. Even if the other person is not specifically knowledgeable of body language, he will pick up vibes or feelings from our gestures, especially if they seem to conflict with what we are saying. He will then be receiving mixed messages. Knowledge of body language will enhance our own self-expression as well as help us to better understand the needs and desires of others.

● ● ● ● ●

As managers, it is important to sense when an employee may be defensive, angry, or frustrated so that we can take action to build and/or restore trust. We can also watch our body language to ensure that we are giving signals which indicate openness. This will help to maintain and increase cooperation.

● ● ● ● ●

We can increase our employees' effectiveness when we increase their comfort level through giving off positive and reassuring signals. We can encourage an employee's full expression with a nod, a smile and other signs indicating our interest in what he is saying and our willingness to listen.

● ● ● ● ●

In selling, body language tells us how we are doing with the prospect before he responds, if he does. His nod, shaking of his head, raised eyebrow, etc. will help us to adjust or adapt our presentation as appropriate. We are able to monitor his feelings, reactions and attitudes.

● ● ● ● ●

A speaker must depend upon nonverbal feedback to properly read his audience and know whether to change pace, tell a story, keep going, or perhaps stop. Otherwise, he is carrying on a one-way conversation, which will not be as effective as it could.

Chapter 15

Writing

Answer the question: "What is my objective in writing the memo or letter?" Write out what you want your reader to know or be able to do when he has read your communication. This is the purpose.

● ● ● ● ●

The clearer a letter or memo seems, the more time the writer has probably spent on revisions. Reread and edit your first draft from the point of view of your intended reader. Anticipate and answer his questions. If the reader has to reread or is confused by the communication, the less likely you are to achieve your objective.

● ● ● ● ●

Written communications are an extension of your company to the public, suppliers, business associates and customers. It makes good sense to take a little time to sharpen your managers' communicating skills and present the best possible image. Many people you deal with will never see your place of business, but only know about you through your communications.

An otherwise good manager can be held back or, as a minimum, rendered less effective without good writing skills. This is a basic communications tool which can be acquired. It takes a knowledge of the general principles governing good writing and ongoing practice.

● ● ● ● ●

Your letters and memos can either turn people on or off. You can control which it is.

Chapter 16

Reading Books

Just as we must eat regularly to maintain our bodies, so we must also have regular, positive input to maintain our minds. Otherwise, the negatives will get us down. We are bombarded day-in and day-out by negative input from negative people which, if not counteracted with positive input on a regular basis, will take its toll. Therefore, it is important to read powerful, positive books on an ongoing basis.

● ● ● ● ●

Studies, including one by the American Management Association, have shown that 20% of a person's success is due to what he knows about his job and industry but 80% is due to his personal characteristics such as self esteem, motivation and determination. Therefore, reading self-help books is important because it contributes toward our personal growth and development. Not only is this important in career development and advancement, but also in our own personal happiness and success.

● ● ● ● ●

Read and listen to self-help books and tapes. Even if you feel you are already knowledgeable in certain areas, it is still good to refresh your thinking and reinforce what you already know. Sometimes we do not practice what we preach or know. When we are exposed to ideas on a repetitive basis, we are more likely to use them.

• • • • •

Many books say the same things in different words. Perhaps the way an author says something or the examples he uses makes a greater impact even though this may be the third or fourth time we have encountered the same basic ideas. We generally learn through repetition. We learn even faster through action, however. Therefore, if we can take immediate action on positive principles, then we own those principles. That is why it is important to set goals to incorporate into our daily living the principles which are contained in the books we read.

• • • • •

You only keep that which you share and give away. The act of sharing and discussing helps to reinforce the information and makes it even more likely that we will incorporate those principles into our everyday living. It is even better when two or three people who have a common interest or goal read the same book or books and then discuss these. It has a multiplication effect.

• • • • •

When I find a book I particularly like, I will purchase several copies for friends who I feel will enjoy them. I often use these as gifts for special occasions or simply as a friendship gift. It might just change someone's life.

SECTION IV

PROFESSIONAL

Chapter 17

Management

Management is the accomplishment of goals through the most efficient use of available resources, i.e., people, capital, equipment, etc.

● ● ● ● ●

Management assumes that there are well-defined objectives. How can there be efficient management of resources unless we know specifically what we are trying to accomplish? This also allows a manager to be measured by the results he achieves.

● ● ● ● ●

A person's management style should be flexible. No one method is appropriate for all organizations, people, problems, and situations. Difficulty arises when there is a conflict in the managerial method employed and the dynamics of the situation, i.e., having an autocratic leader where the profile of the organization and subordinates calls for a democratic or participative style. This is when morale suffers, employee turnover increases and productivity declines.

In line with good developmental theory, decisions should be made at the lowest possible organizational level, commensurate with the knowledge and skills of the persons involved.

• • • • •

Standardize most actions. This reduces many activities to a routine which allows more time to concentrate on the major items that do require thinking and decision making.

• • • • •

When a problem surfaces, investigate the causes, not to pinpoint blame, but rather to determine how you can modify your operation to preclude a recurrence of that problem. This ensures that you are not continually reinventing the wheel.

• • • • •

Hire persons of excellence by administering a screening/psychological test to ensure the best possible match between the candidate and the position. Then provide your employees with their responsibilities in the form of written job descriptions and manuals. After a period of training, test them to ensure that they understand the procedures and then provide good supervision with competitive compensation and abundant recognition.

• • • • •

As people grow in their positions and/or are promoted, they gain self-esteem because they feel successful. Promoting from within is also a great morale builder as employees see others within the organization promoted. This gives them hope for promotion, if that is their goal.

We can be successful only to the extent that we can help our employees and company owners accomplish their goals.

• • • • •

We do not have unlimited time and unlimited access to all relevant information. If we did, a decision would not be necessary because it would be obvious.

• • • • •

When we encourage delegation of responsibility, which includes ensuring that the person is capable of handling the additional responsibility and has sufficient training and ongoing guidance, it allows the person to grow in his position and to assume increasingly higher levels of responsibility which then makes him a likely candidate for promotion.

• • • • •

Effective delegation depends more on leadership skills than position power. Leaders who delegate wisely are the ones who develop capable subordinates. It's the best sign that they themselves are ready to move ahead.

• • • • •

Delegation is the foundation of organization. It is the means of multiplying effectiveness in getting results through others.

• • • • •

The delegation of authority is the means whereby a manager extends his influence and control and becomes capable of assuming greater responsibility.

Whenever we begin to measure something and pinpoint responsibility, it automatically improves. Then we have a handle by which to do many other things such as recognition, feedback, compensation and evaluation. When something becomes measurable, it automatically increases. For example, when we began measuring resident satisfaction via service reply cards, satisfaction improved. People concentrate on that which is measured and reported, especially if it involves recognition and compensation.

● ● ● ● ●

Scheduling proceduralizes that which comes naturally to persons who are organized. However, with a formal, written schedule, even greater efficiency results. In addition, it affords the supervisor the opportunity to better control the person's work and therefore improve his efficiency.

● ● ● ● ●

Even in our daily personal lives, scheduling assists us in the form of a simple "to do" list. The mere writing of a list of the things to do will help ensure that they will be accomplished. Obviously, the more sophisticated the scheduling system becomes, the more efficient we will become. For example, attaching priorities to each item along with estimated timetables will enhance the value of a "to do" list as a scheduling tool.

● ● ● ● ●

Growth for growth's sake has never been one of our objectives. Our hallmark is quality.

● ● ● ● ●

Getting to the top of an industry isn't the real criterion for success. Staying there is.

We believe that when we share information, we get as much or more in return. This sharing helps to create valuable dialogue that can benefit all those who participate in an industry.

• • • • •

Through developing standard operating procedures, we have enabled our people to perform at maximum levels of efficiency by showing them the best way, based upon experience, to perform their job responsibilities. They don't have to learn through years of experience and through extensive outside training before being qualified to perform. In effect, they receive on-the-job guidance by following the procedures until it becomes habit. However, it is not rote following of procedures. We carefully explain the rationale for each procedure and allow individual variations within a loosely structured plan. It is this plan, however, which ensures that no one will deviate from the correct path unless and until a better way is found.

• • • • •

I believe a business executive not only has a moral obligation to belong to and support an organization serving the needs and protecting the interests of his industry, but it is also wise from a strictly business standpoint. And, it can be personally enjoyable and rewarding.

Chapter 18

Qualities Of A Manager

A successful manager must have single-mindedness of purpose. He must know what his goals are and have a strong desire to accomplish them. He will therefore more effectively utilize various areas of his endeavors to impact the attainment of the goal. He will achieve a high degree of unity in his affairs.

●●●●●

When a person is motivated by a specific goal, he will have a high degree of determination and will not be likely to quit when he encounters a setback. He will want to learn from the experience and be more effective the next time.

●●●●●

A successful manager must make a commitment to work the hours necessary to carry out the plan of action to accomplish the goals. This commitment involves both time and energy and whatever other resources are necessary. If the desire is strong enough and the goal is attractive enough, then the person is willing to put in the hours and does not consider it as work.

A successful manager must have a positive mental attitude, which means that he is open to suggestions and ideas and is flexible enough to incorporate the ideas of others into his master plan in accomplishing the goal. He does not have egotistical pride of authorship but is willing to listen, absorb and apply the ideas and suggestions of others into his plan of action. He is a possibility thinker. He thinks, creates and looks for opportunities and ways to improve the method that he is using in accomplishing his goals. He is results-oriented and willing to adjust the plan if it furthers the attainment of the goal.

● ● ● ● ●

Success in management takes a definite goal, a detailed and timetabled plan of action, hard work, a positive mental attitude, desire, a high degree of organization and determination.

● ● ● ● ●

A successful manager must be highly organized. He must develop a plan of action designed to accomplish, step-by-step, the goals which are the measure of his success. This must also involve careful time management techniques. Time is a person's most critical resource and it is imperative that it be utilized to maximum advantage for the attainment of the stated goal.

● ● ● ● ●

A manager must be self-motivated. If it is true that the organization or department is only the lengthened shadow of its leader, then it is important that its leader be a self-motivated goal setter. He must be up when everyone else is down. He must be able to lift others not only by what he says but in the way he acts and conducts himself.

● ● ● ● ●

A manager must be a good listener.

A manager must be a good communicator, both verbally and in writing. This is important, not only within the organization, but also in representing his organization to others – the public, suppliers, bankers, customers, etc.

● ● ● ● ●

A manager should possess good human relations skills to enable him to deal effectively with all levels – superiors, subordinates and peers. Management most often involves doing things with and through people. Therefore, the way a manager interacts with other people will determine, to a large measure, his success.

● ● ● ● ●

Past performance is an excellent guide to future performance because habits, once formed, continue, unless there is strong, motivated action to change.

● ● ● ● ●

When hiring a manager or someone you plan to develop into a manager, you can determine whether he possesses the necessary qualities by closely scrutinizing his past behavioral characteristics as evidenced by his personal and professional performance – his track record. After closely researching these areas, you can use that information in conducting an in-depth, personal interview by asking significant, open-ended questions.

● ● ● ● ●

There is a difference between someone who has ten years of experience and one who has only one year's experience repeated ten times. The latter individual never learns from his experience, but is destined to repeat his mistakes. The successful manager extracts every lesson possible from his experience so his skills and performance continue to improve. He is a lifelong learner, never satisfied with his skills or knowledge.

● ● ● ● ●

A manager should continue to improve his skills through education and experience. He should be able to make his experience a meaningful lesson by learning not only from his successes, but, more importantly, from his failures. He should analyze what went wrong, why and how it can be prevented in the future.

● ● ● ● ●

A manager must possess integrity. Over the long run, his associates will come to understand whether he possesses this quality and it will go a long way in determining whether they develop and maintain respect for his leadership. Without respect, generally earned based upon competence and integrity, he cannot long be a successful manager. Integrity is the foundation upon which his skills and abilities are built.

Chapter 19

Time Management

Time management begins with goal setting. It is impossible to organize time unless we know what we are organizing to do or accomplish. Otherwise, what difference does it make how we spend our time?

●　●　●　●　●

Often we say we wish we had more time, more time to start a new hobby or read a few more books. We can give ourselves the time to do the things we really want to do if we set goals, prioritize and organize.

●　●　●　●　●

Time is the essence of life. It is our only basic, irreplaceable, diminishing resource. How we spend our time determines the quality of our life. How we spend our time at work determines how productive we are and, therefore, how much we earn.

●　●　●　●　●

Everyone has the same amount of time — 24 hours per day. The difference is how each utilizes the time.

The higher we move up the organizational ladder, the more critical it is to use our time effectively. There are infinite demands on the finite time that is available. How well we organize to cope with those demands determines our effectiveness.

● ● ● ● ●

As a by-product of the identification of our values and goals, we will make the time necessary to accomplish those goals by eliminating any activities, people and organizations which do not contribute toward that accomplishment.

● ● ● ● ●

We generally establish the working mode of our organization. If our people see that we are organized, they are more likely to follow the example.

● ● ● ● ●

If we develop a plan and work it, our business associates will begin to respect the fact that our time is organized and will be less likely to continually interrupt. Instead, they will be more likely to accumulate questions for one scheduled meeting where more can be accomplished on an organized basis rather than with a series of time consuming interruptions throughout the day. In many cases, they will devise their own solutions to problems rather than continually interrupting us.

● ● ● ● ●

Try to do things immediately because it takes much less time than to put them off and have to review each item again in order to do it later.

The key idea in time management is PRIORITIES. It is not enough to use a "to do" list indiscriminately. Each of our activities should be prioritized in the order of its importance. We should begin with the first item and not go to the second until we have finished the first and so on. Too often, however, we spend 80% of our time on that which accomplishes 20% of the job.

● ● ● ● ●

The most difficult part of any job is getting started.

● ● ● ● ●

Each piece of paper should be handled only once with any indicated action taken at that time. It is a waste of time to review the same paper twice.

● ● ● ● ●

By the end of each day, all incoming mail should be processed.

● ● ● ● ●

Paperwork should be done on a daily basis to prevent a buildup and also to preclude forgetting the information that is to be put on reports.

● ● ● ● ●

Do not mistake activity for accomplishment. By planning and organizing, this is not likely to happen. Every action will be effective because it will be goal-directed.

At the beginning of each day, we should have a priority listing of those items which are to be accomplished and then accomplish them in that order.

● ● ● ● ●

A plan is important even though it may be subject to change. In fact, the more subject it is to change, the more important it is to have a plan to ensure accomplishment of major objectives.

Chapter 20

Business Practices

If you have something to do, do it now. It is a safe bet that there will be additional actions to be taken tomorrow and the next day. Therefore, do not put off until later items which can be done now. Chances are they can be done more quickly and efficiently immediately while you are thinking about them. Otherwise, you will put them aside and then have to start thinking about them all over again to initiate the action. DO IT NOW! You will be amazed at the amount you can accomplish by following this philosophy.

● ● ● ● ●

Unless we are out in the field from time to time, mixing with our employees and clients, it is too easy to lose contact with the real world and make decisions without benefit of up-to-date accurate information. We must maintain the feel of the field. Even if information reaches us relatively undistorted, it is still not the same as our first-hand observations. We are more experienced in the organization and able to view details, events and people from a greater perspective. Therefore, we should be able to see things that would not be readily apparent to middle and first line supervisory personnel who do not have the years of experience or the benefit of our broad based knowledge. This also presents an excellent opportunity for us to teach and instruct our managers by example. And, of course, there is the important side benefit of having the front line people see the head person.

• • • • •

Spend time with your employees. Give them a chance to talk. You might learn something. Also, it gives them a feeling of importance. But, be careful to ask only non-intimidating, open-end questions and *listen*.

• • • • •

Always try to make use of the talents and abilities of others in a constructive way. It not only improves overall productivity but also helps to develop the individual by assisting him in tapping his resources and abilities.

• • • • •

Involve an employee in the decision making process. Let him participate in evolving the solution to a problem in which he is involved. He may provide valuable input because he is on the scene and will be more receptive to the solution if he helped to develop it. In addition, he will have a vested interest in ensuring the success of the solution when implemented.

• • • • •

A supervisor should not state that a procedure must be performed because someone else, presumably higher up in the company, said so. This makes the supervisor look ineffective and also diminishes the probability that the directive will be effectively performed.

When giving directions, give the purpose and rationale. A person will be more likely to carry them out and perhaps even suggest a better way of accomplishing the purpose.

● ● ● ● ●

Only 20% of a job is giving instructions on what to do but 80% is follow-up to ensure that the actions are taken.

● ● ● ● ●

When we go into a meeting or talk with another person with the probability that some action will be agreed upon, we should always have a pencil and paper so that these items can be written down immediately. With so many things to do and as much information as we must remember, it is essential that we write out actions which we plan to take.

● ● ● ● ●

When we ask someone to take some action, we should ensure that he commits it to writing. Otherwise, it will probably not be accomplished. The fact that he does write it down increases the probability that he will eventually do it but does not, in itself, ensure that it will be done. Follow-up is necessary.

● ● ● ● ●

Don't assume anything. It is the lesser of two evils to cover subject matter that an employee may already know than to omit something that he may not know. It is better to err on the part of over-covering than under-covering. Furthermore, we learn through repetition.

If a direction or instruction can be misunderstood or interpreted wrongly, it will be. Therefore, when communicating either in writing or verbally, it should be clear, concise and specific. As much as possible, directions and procedures should be stated in a step-by-step form.

● ● ● ● ●

Every communication should be legible and contain simple, clear, concise statements. It should be typed, if possible, and dated.

● ● ● ● ●

Forms should be used as much as possible to eliminate extraneous information and to preclude forgetting information essential to covering the subject matter. Forms merely require that blanks be filled in and are preferable to memos for transmitting information. They also provide a blueprint to follow in accomplishing the task.

● ● ● ● ●

Each of us should develop and utilize a plan so that there is no wasted motion. We should know each day, week and month what needs to be done to bring us closer to our goals.

● ● ● ● ●

Though we learn through repetition, we learn faster and better through action.

Chapter 21

Hiring, Selection, And Compensation

The key to increased productivity and profits in business is in proper employee selection and then efficient, ongoing management of those employees. They represent our greatest reservoir for increased productivity and profits. If we can somehow become more scientific in the selection of those employees and then more effective in their ongoing management, we will be successful.

• • • • •

The initial challenge in recruiting is in proper employee selection. We must match the job and the employee. There are two job elements which must first be considered and determined. The first is the technical requirements and the second is the personal characteristics required for performing that job. In other words, what technical qualifications and personal characteristics should the applicant possess to maximize the chance for success in that position? No amount of training will overcome poor employee selection. We must hire those individuals who are most qualified from a technical and personal standpoint.

• • • • •

The objective is to identify the qualities which are most likely to produce success in a specific job. The task is then to locate an individual

88 | FLYING TO YOUR SUCCESS!

whose behavioral characteristics, as evidenced by his past performance and test results, most nearly coincide with these qualities. A high correlation between the qualities required for successful performance of the job and the qualities possessed by an individual is most likely to result in successful placement. This will maximize the job comfort level of an employee and be more likely to lead to success in the job.

● ● ● ● ●

The biggest challenge is in determining the personal characteristics required for successful accomplishment of the job responsibilities and measuring whether the person possesses these to the necessary degree. This is not only more difficult than the technical but also more important. Studies have shown that only 20% of a person's success is due to his technical knowledge whereas 80% is due to his personal characteristics such as self-motivation, time management skills, human relations skills, etc. Besides, the technical skills can be more easily increased. Personal characteristics change very slowly, if at all.

● ● ● ● ●

Test results are only indicators of certain characteristics and should not be considered absolute and final predictors of performance. In addition, tests do not make the decision. The interviewer, who should be the person for whom the applicant will work, is vested with that responsibility. Test results are merely one tool used in the selection process and are used to supplement basic impressions gathered from an in-depth personal interview, background checks, personal knowledge of performance, etc. It is one of the inputs to be used in making a hiring decision and not the entire basis for a decision.

● ● ● ● ●

Across-the-board wage increases tend to breed mediocrity. When everyone is paid the same, any possible striving for excellence is discouraged. Everyone's output tends to decline to the lowest level.

The incentive system takes us one step further than the merit increase system and even more closely correlates to the person's productivity. It removes, to a great extent, the judgment factor where a person's increase may not be exactly commensurate with productivity but only roughly so — based upon an evaluation which hopefully reflects his actual performance level.

• • • • •

In the selling profession when a person is on a straight commission basis, you have the purest example of incentive pay. The person's income exactly reflects his performance. This, in fact, is the greatest security. Many people feel that a salesperson's income is subject to fluctuation and they are, therefore, insecure. However, when a person's income directly reflects his productivity, he has security because he can go anywhere with his productivity and earn income. When a person on a straight salary basis is released or leaves his present job, it is more difficult for him to find employment elsewhere, especially at the same pay because the pay probably reflected a combination of seniority and, to a much lesser extent, performance. His so-called security lasts only as long as some entrepreneur, who is operating on a strictly incentive basis himself, desires his services. Also, because he is incurring no risk (his absolute "security"), his pay is not as high as one who is willing to assume some risk.

• • • • •

People resent being paid the same and getting the same increases as others who are not putting out the same effort or securing the same results. Soon their initiative and drive recede as they see that the benefits are not commensurate with their output.

• • • • •

Not only does incentive pay motivate a person to produce more but he is also more satisfied with his work. A person tends to be more satisfied when he is being productive. Time passes faster, he enjoys his work more and earns more. Straight hourly wages generally lead to job dissatisfaction and about 50% turnover. This conclusion was reached after a year-long study of two factories — one operating on an incentive pay basis and one on an hourly basis.

● ● ● ● ●

I am always suspicious of someone who would prefer having a straight wage (salary or hourly) compared with incentive pay or a combination of wage and incentive pay. It is an indication that he does not have the confidence or drive to risk the possibility of lower pay compared with straight salary versus the upside possibility of a much higher incentive reward for outstanding performance and results. The American capitalist system was built by entrepreneurs who were willing to take that risk to the highest degree.

Chapter 22

Employee Motivation

Since the greatest potential gain in productivity is with people, it makes sense to provide the means by which they can become more efficient and productive.

● ● ● ● ●

The key idea in motivation is FEEDBACK. People must know their responsibilities (job description) and must be advised how their performance compares. This is the key to motivation — providing objectives and feedback. This feedback can be in the form of periodic performance appraisals, ongoing recognition, and/or constructive criticism when the person is off track.

● ● ● ● ●

We owe it to our people to communicate their specific responsibilities and to provide feedback on how well they are accomplishing these. In fact, this is what motivation is all about.

If employees don't have personal goals, it is impossible to show them any relationship between the company and personal goals; that person cannot be motivated. Therefore, it is important to help your employees set goals so you can show that relationship. They must then set up a plan of action to accomplish both.

● ● ● ● ●

When a person identifies his personal goals with the goals of an organization, an enormous release of human energy, creativity and loyalty results. People are motivated by what they will get out of work or any other activity and not by what someone else wants. They are motivated for their own reasons – not ours.

● ● ● ● ●

Employees must understand how they can accomplish their own personal and professional objectives by helping the company accomplish its objectives. People do not work simply because they are interested in helping the company succeed. A person is interested in helping the company accomplish its objectives when he clearly understands that he will come closer to accomplishing his objectives when that happens. There must be a tie-in of objectives.

● ● ● ● ●

Employees are motivated when they understand their share of the company goal and when they are recognized and compensated based upon accomplishment. Your employees must not only know what their share of the company's goal is but also receive feedback concerning accomplishment. This is what really motivates a person – having specific objectives and getting feedback on accomplishment of those objectives and being recognized and compensated in proportion to that accomplishment.

The only thing that you or anyone else can do to motivate another is to encourage and perhaps assist a person in setting goals and then show the tie-in with company goals. You can then provide the positive environment conducive to effective work, i.e., training, direction, recognition, compensation, and managing with human relations skills.

● ● ● ● ●

Though compensation is secondary to recognition and other factors in motivation, it is nonetheless important and must be considered. One way to clearly demonstrate a tie-in is through a bonus arrangement which rewards the employee when he accomplishes the specific objectives for which he is responsible.

● ● ● ● ●

Occasionally, someone will ask me to come to his place of business to "motivate my people. My sales people are dragging and not selling anything." My response is always, "I'm sorry, but I can't motivate your people nor anyone else for that matter." I go on to state that no one, either within or outside the organization, can motivate his people. It has to come from within the employee and stems from his own goals.

● ● ● ● ●

No amount of follow-up or management scrutiny will overcome a lack of employee motivation which occurs when a person has no goals and/or does not see a relationship between his goals and the company's goals.

● ● ● ● ●

Money is no longer the only, or even the most important, motivation. Employees must derive satisfaction from the work itself. Otherwise, their morale will suffer and they will not perform at a high level of efficiency.

Chapter 23

Customer Service

Everyone in an organization must know that customer service is a high priority.

● ● ● ● ●

Customer service must be established as a philosophy, policy and standard operating procedure. If we leave it alone, it will get worse.

● ● ● ● ●

Customer service is a mind set which starts at the top and is transmitted as a value throughout the rest of the organization to the front line. It must be established as an integral part of the performance evaluation and compensation system. It becomes ingrained in the corporate culture.

● ● ● ● ●

Customer service is an attitude that must begin at the top. Management must establish customer service as a high priority item, then transmit that attitude to the front line where contact with the customer takes place. This attitude must be reinforced by customer service training, establishing specific goals, measuring accomplishment of those goals, providing feedback on that accomplishment, recognition, evaluation, and compensation. Customer service must be more than merely lip service.

● ● ● ● ●

We communicate company and individual values, not only by what we say but, most importantly, by what we do. The more dramatic the action, the more of an impact it makes. These stories become embellished through the years, further reinforcing the lessons demonstrated. It becomes part of the company folklore.

● ● ● ● ●

Management must personally be involved and committed to customer service. This can be accomplished in many ways such as taking phone calls from irate customers and visits to the field. In other words, involvement. How we spend our personal time demonstrates our commitment, our values and our priorities. We cannot say one thing and do something else.

● ● ● ● ●

We must make sure that our front line people are paid commensurate with their skill level and importance to the organization. Often, these are the lowest paid, most inexperienced people in the organization. The morale tends to be the lowest and the turnover greatest. Yet, these are the people who carry the image of our organization to our customers.

● ● ● ● ●

How people perceive us determines how they react to us. If we put out bad vibes, then we will be perceived as an unfriendly person, one to be avoided if at all possible. This happens within 30 seconds of the initial encounter. This can result in lost sales.

We must check our attitude and that of our employees before they deal with customers to ensure that there is a smile, pleasant voice, enthusiasm, a knowledge of the job and a willingness to be of service to customers. We must engrain into the minds and hearts of our employees that the customer is our job, not an interruption to our job. Without customers, there would be no jobs. The reports, discussions with supervisors and co-workers and everything else are purely secondary to serving customers.

● ● ● ● ●

The ultimate motivation for providing good customer service is the internal satisfaction which people receive because they are doing a good job. That is the internal reward which, in the final analysis and in the long run, is the ongoing motivation for good customer service.

● ● ● ● ●

Customer handling skills are more important than technical skills because we can learn the latter more easily than we can change the former, which reflect an attitude and is more difficult to change.

● ● ● ● ●

When a customer feels that he is courteously treated and appreciated, he will not only be more satisfied but also be more receptive to any additional services that we offer, to repeat business and to referring others to our company.

● ● ● ● ●

Many customers don't bother to tell us there is something wrong. They simply stop doing business with us. We should be thankful when a customer takes the trouble to let us know that he has a problem. It usually means that we have a problem.

Unfortunately, "minimum shaft expectation" all too accurately describes the frame of mind of people attempting to get any kind of service.

• • • • •

Substantial amounts of money are spent in getting a customer into our place of business. This can be wasted without a commitment to retain the new or established customer through consistent and good customer service by our employees. People select businesses where they feel wanted and cared about. This must be transmitted by the front line customer contact personnel. These are the people who have the greatest direct impact upon our customers. Somehow we must create an increased awareness and commitment to good customer service.

Chapter 24

Work

When we do the type of work with which we are most comfortable and that we enjoy the most, we are more likely to be successful.

● ● ● ● ●

If you can't find an existing job that calls for the type of talent and enthusiasm that you have, then go out and create one or reshape an existing one, perhaps even the one you now occupy. Often, a change in job is not necessary, only a change in attitude. Sometimes we can inject new life and excitement into our present job by setting and accomplishing goals.

● ● ● ● ●

Don't say that there is no job that pays you for doing what you enjoy. If you do enough introspection, you can find those activities that you are best suited for, most comfortable with and that you have fun doing. That is what you should be doing for a living.

Not only will we be successful from a financial standpoint by doing what we enjoy but life in general will be more positive, rewarding and fulfilling.

• • • • •

People often comment about "paying the price of success." I think of it in terms of "enjoying the price," especially if we are "working" at something we enjoy.

• • • • •

Any money and happiness will come as a by-product of loving what we do and putting everything into it.

• • • • •

Separating one's work life from private life tends to be regarded by our society as a good and necessary thing. We often hear "Leave the job at the office." But is it possible? Probably not.

• • • • •

My wish for you is not that you work longer or harder hours, but rather shorter, more productive hours toward the attainment of your personal and professional goals.

• • • • •

Within 30 days after he retired as head football coach of the University of Alabama, the legendary Bear Bryant died. Football was everything to him. He did not ensure that there was something else to fill that void. Unfortunately for many, when work is completed so is life. When one type of work is finished or when we retire, we must find a substitute.

Well meaning friends, relatives and co-workers may advise the workaholic to "take it easy" and get away for a while. They recommend a long vacation in which the workaholic could relax on the beach. In fact, that is not what the workaholic wants or needs. This is the surest way to damage him both physically and emotionally. He does not need to get away from it all because he is enjoying it all. The cure would be worse than the disease. In such an extended, inactive vacation, he would be totally at loose ends and distressed.

● ● ● ● ●

Rather than a futile attempt to "cure" the workaholic, you might try to assist and guide him in channeling his efforts in a positive, productive (in your terms) manner both at home and/or at work.

● ● ● ● ●

The workaholic is upbeat and positive and tends to wake up with enthusiasm and an uncommon expectation for the day. Some of his positivism may rub off on his friends and family members which is a good by-product. Unfortunately, in most cases, it is not enough to nourish the relationship. Those who remain in a relationship with a workaholic must find their own self-sustaining activities during the long hours that the workaholic will be involved in his own pursuits. They must have high self esteem and low affection requirements. Most, however, cannot accommodate the extreme lifestyle of the workaholic.

● ● ● ● ●

No matter where you see a workaholic — in an airport, in a doctor's waiting room, at a stoplight in his automobile, anywhere — they are always working. They may be reading, dictating, listening to a tape, or engaged in intense thinking about a problem or opportunity. There is almost no wasted effort in the direction of his objective.

Instead of using up energy, workaholics' activities actually generate additional energy which allows them to work hour after hour, long after their peers have left for the day. They are intense, energetic, competitive and driven. The intensity of a workaholic is actually inspiring.

● ● ● ● ●

Workaholics are not the unhappy and always harried lot as they are usually pictured. Instead, they tend to be happy individuals who have a tremendous zest for life. They tirelessly pursue their interests and love every minute of it. That is why it is so difficult for them to tear themselves away from those interests to engage in the normally accepted activities such as vacations, relaxation and sports.

● ● ● ● ●

People often put down workaholics because of their alleged addiction to work. They support this contention with many supposed ills, both to the workaholic and others. However, the only valid scientific study of workaholics was performed by Dr. Marilyn Machlowitz who found that, for the most part, workaholics are happy, healthy and productive. Contrary to popular belief, workaholics are actually healthier and happier, and live longer than the general population.

Cha\

Selling

104 | FLYING TO YOUR SUCCESS!
A salesperson should listen carefully...
A salesperson does not usually the second...
reason given, but usually an...
one reason given for doing...
first reason given for...
cially acceptable up...
one that is based...

We are all in the sel...   ...g his
employees, the boss and hi...   ...selling the
beloved; the student is selling h...   ...the job applicant
is selling himself to the prospe...   ...d he, in turn, is selling
his company to the prospective e...

● ● ● ● ●

Not only are we all in the selling business, but that business is of critical importance to our economy and the management profession. Selling is the life blood of our economy. It starts the production lines rolling.

● ● ● ● ●

We must be highly organized, including effective time management. A salesperson's investment is his time.

● ● ● ● ●

There is no substitute for going out and beating the bushes. To sell, we must make calls, otherwise known as prospecting. If we are afraid to use the telephone, the only way to overcome that fear is to start phoning.

the prospect to find the real
. That reason is seldom the first
or subsequent reason. Generally, the
thing is the one that sounds good — the so-
The second one is usually the real reason — the
more selfish motives.

● ● ● ● ●

Selling is not converting people to our way of thinking, but rather to our way of feeling. That's why we've got to believe what we do and, as a corollary, we've got to do what we believe.

● ● ● ● ●

We must appeal not only to the logic of a prospect but also his emotions. Most buying decisions, in the final analysis, are emotional.

● ● ● ● ●

We must believe in ourselves and in our product or service.

About The Author

Frank Basile has presented over 750 speeches, seminars and workshops across the United States and Canada in the last ten years. He is former president of the Indiana Chapter of the National Speakers Association (NSA) and holds the designation of Certified Speaking Professional (CSP). He received the Toastmasters International Communication and Leadership Award for 1983.

He has authored ten books, including PROFESSIONAL MULTI-HOUSING MANAGEMENT, which is the official textbook for the Registered Apartment Manager (RAM) course of the National Association of Home Builders (NAHB). His first book, COME FLY WITH ME, has sold over 23,000 copies, primarily in connection with his speeches.

Frank writes a column on management for the INDIANAPOLIS BUSINESS JOURNAL. He has written more than 400 articles for many national and regional publications such as MARKETING TIMES, official publication of Sales and Marketing Executives International (SMEI), and JOURNAL OF PROPERTY MANAGEMENT, official publication of the Institute of Real Estate Management (IREM).

He is vice president of the Gene B. Glick Co., Inc. with responsibility for the company's 20,000 apartments and 650 employees in 13 states. Frank is also president of Charisma Publications, Inc., which handles the sales of his books, tapes, manuals, speeches and seminars. He is a Field Manager for Performax Systems, Inc. He was formerly General Field Manager for the Indianapolis District of the Ford Motor Company where he was responsible for the sales and profitability of 175 Ford dealers in Indiana.

Within the apartment management industry, he is a member of both the National Faculty and the Academy of Authors of IREM and is a Certified Property Manager (CPM). He is former national vice president of the National Apartment Association, former president of the Apartment Association of Indiana and former chairman of the RAM Board of Governors of the NAHB. He received the PROFESSIONAL BUILDER Apartment Management Achievement Award in 1983 and the Registered Apartment Manager (RAM) of the Year Award in 1984.

His civic activities include former board member of the Better Business Bureau of Central Indiana, former president of the Indianapolis Free University, former president of Indianapolis Sales and Marketing Executives (SME), and former member of the Board of Trustees of All Souls Unitarian Church.

He is a graduate of Tulane University in New Orleans where he graduated as class valedictorian and student body president. He is listed in WHO'S WHO IN THE MIDWEST, WHO'S WHO IN REAL ESTATE, WHO'S WHO IN FINANCE AND INDUSTRY, and WHO'S WHO IN SALES AND MARKETING.

Besides speaking and writing, Frank's hobbies include ballroom dancing, bicycling, exercising, dining out, conversations with friends, attending movies and plays, and reading articles and books.

THE INDIANAPOLIS STAR
Sunday, March 22, 1981

Recognize With Praise As Well As Raise

By James L. Adams

Companies that want to increase productivity must make employees understand the connections between worker's personal goals and corporate goals, Frank M. Basile says.

"People do things for their own reasons and not for ours," says this well-known, local motivational expert. "We must help our employees understand that when they help the company accomplish its goals, they in turn will come closer to accomplishing their own goals."

An understanding of this relationship, he says, would make employees more enthusiastic about their part in helping the company's overall productivity.

Management must spend time with its employees, Basile says, to help them feel that they are an integral part of the organization, that what they do matters to the company and that when they perform well, they are recognized with praise, as well as raises.

"Not by bread alone does man live, but by having positive feedback and recognition from others, especially supervisory personnel."

Basile's ability to clarify those relationships and point out the best ways to motivate people have brought him plenty of positive feedback and recognition.

Officially, he's vice-president of Gene Glick Management Corporation, a job that involves overseeing 20,000 apartments in 13 states. Unofficially, he is Indianapolis' best-known proponent of positive thinking and personal motivation through his roles as lecturer, author, teacher and philanthropist.

"If I can change someone's life to be more positive, his job more enjoyable, his self-respect greater—that's what it's all about for me."

When he is not in the office or in the field supervising the activities of 650 employees, the 41 year-old New Orleans native uses his "spare" time for speaking engagements and writing books, articles and columns on such diverse subjects as personal motivation, goal setting, time management, stress, selling techniques and real estate management. Basile may be the state's most prolific speaker. He gave 85 speeches in 1980 and 200 in the last three years.

He also finds time for teaching. For the last five years, he has taught a salesmanship course, sponsored by the Indianapolis Sales and Marketing Executives, at Butler University. He teaches another class at Free University during each two-month semester without compensation.

In recognition of his numerous articles on salesmanship in MARKETING TIMES, the official publication of Sales and Marketing Executives International, the magazine named him one of seven national "Movers and Shakers" in the sales and marketing field in 1980.

The best-known of his nine books is COME FLY WITH ME, a guide to accomplishing personal and professional goals. "What I really do is use the books to reinforce the message. It's been established that people will forget most of what they've heard in three days if they don't write it down or have it in writing."

Basile's basic speech teaches motivational techniques by which people can improve their attitudes and reach their goals. If the letters and calls he receives are any indication, his one-day workshops and 45 minute talks are having some impact.

Someone writes to say he has accomplished a goal because he followed through on Basile's advice. The wife of a mayor of a small southern Indiana town calls to say that she has decided to return to college to get her degree because she attended his workshop. A letter comes from a businessman who says his sales increased 25% the six months after Basile's presentation to his salespeople.

Those calls and letters, along with the knowledge "that I have been instrumental in encouraging or motivating another human being toward a fuller, happier and more productive life, are the best rewards," Basile says.

Reprinted from:
THE INDIANAPOLIS STAR
Sunday, March 22, 1981.

ORDER FORM
CHARISMA PUBLICATIONS, INC.
BOOKS AND TAPES
by
Frank Basile

BOOKS	PRICE	COPIES	TOTAL
FLYING TO YOUR SUCCESS (Personal & Professional Development)	$ 6.00 X	_____	= $ _____
COME FLY WITH ME (Goal Setting)	5.00 X	_____	= $ _____
BUILD A BETTER YOU – STARTING NOW (Personal Growth)	14.00 X	_____	= $ _____
THE MAGNIFICENT MOTIVATORS (Motivation & Achievement)	15.00 X	_____	= $ _____
PROFESSIONAL MULTIHOUSING MANAGEMENT (NAHB Textbook)	30.00 X	_____	= $ _____
MULTIHOUSING MANAGEMENT: ADVANCED PRINCIPLES AND PRACTICES (NAHB Textbook)	24.00 X	_____	= $ _____

CASSETTE TAPE
COME FLY WITH ME (Motivation & Goal Setting)   6.00 X_____ = $ _____

VIDEO TAPE (VHS)
RENTING IS SELLING (Includes Study Guide. NAHB Production)   45.00 X_____ = $ _____

OTHER
PERSONAL PROFILE BOOKLET (Personality Analysis)   8.00 X_____ = $ _____

TOTAL _____ $ _____

☐ Payment enclosed   ☐ VISA   ☐ MasterCard   ☐ Invoice me

Account No. _____ Expiration Date _____

Please return order form and payment to: CHARISMA PUBLICATIONS, INC.
P.O. Box 40321
Indianapolis, IN 46240
(317) 259-8743

☐ Please send information on Frank Basile's programs, topics and fees.

Name _____ Company Name _____

Street/Box No. _____ City _____

State _____ Zip Code _____ Phone ( ) _____

Date _____ Signature _____

GOAL

_____

_____

TIMETABLE

_____

PLAN OF ACTION

_____

_____

_____

Frank Basile
(317) 259-8743
P.O. BOX 40321 ● INDIANAPOLIS, IN 46240

GOAL

_____

_____

TIMETABLE

_____

PLAN OF ACTION

_____

_____

_____

Frank Basile
(317) 259-8743
P.O. BOX 40321 ● INDIANAPOLIS, IN 46240

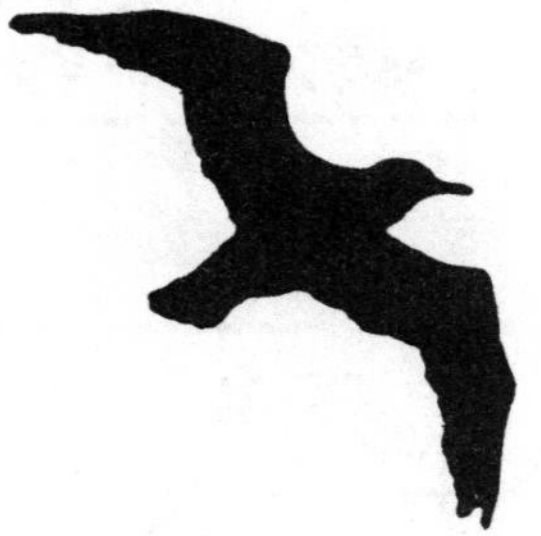

NOTES

NOTES